Oxford Discover Grammar

2nd

1

Helen Casey

OXFORD

UNIVERSITY PRESS

OXFORD
UNIVERSITY PRESS

Great Clarendon Street, Oxford, OX2 6DP, United Kingdom

Oxford University Press is a department of the University of Oxford.
It furthers the University's objective of excellence in research, scholarship,
and education by publishing worldwide. Oxford is a registered trade
mark of Oxford University Press in the UK and in certain other countries

ISBN: 978 0 19 405265 8

Printed in China

This book is printed on paper from certified and well-managed sources

ACKNOWLEDGEMENTS

Back cover photograph: Oxford University Press building/David Fisher

Illustrations by: **Mark Brierley/Beehive Illustration** 29, 30 (Exam Time), 57,
66, 79; **Craig Cameron/Beehive** pp.17, 31, 35, 58, 71, 80; **Nigel Dobbyn/
Beehive Illustration** in the style of Mark Brierley/Beehive Illustration pp.5,
6, 7, 12; **Clonefront Entertainment/Beehive Illustration** in the style of
Craig Cameron/Beehive Illustration pp.4, 5, 9, 10, 11; **Dusan Pavlic/Beehive
Illustration** pp.8, 18, 19, 20, 21 24, 25, 28, 30, 33, 37, 38, 42, 46, 51, 55, 60, 61,
64, 65, 73, 74, 87, 91.

*The publisher would like to thank the following for their permission to reproduce
photographs*: **Alamy** pp.13 (Nico/T.M.O.Pictures, scouts planting tree/Blend
Images), 14 (girl scouts/van Hilversum), 15 (canoe lesson/Neil McAllister, girl
scouts/van Hilversum), 16 (Ella/van Hilversum, Nico/T.M.O.Pictures), 22 (lizard/
Frans Lanting Studio, polar bears/Design Pics Inc., woodpecker/srijanrc birds),
41 (ranger/Bill Bachmann), 43 (bear/Alaska Stock, ranger/Bill Bachmann),
49 (cars/Conrad Elias), 62 (scientists/US Coast Guard Photo), 67(circus camp/
Tony Gwynne), 70 (circus camp/Tony Gwynne), 75 (narrowboat/Anna Stowe),
78 (boys/Ethel Wolvovitz, band/LOOK Die Bildagentur der Fotografen GmbH),
79 (boys/Ethel Wolvovitz, band/LOOK Die Bildagentur der Fotografen GmbH,
seller/Fireflash), 82 (drumming/Gallo Images, theatre/UpperCut Images),
88 (boy/Andrea Matone), 90 (plant pot/Design Pics Inc); **Corbis** pp.68 (boys/
Ron Nickel); **Getty** pp.7 (3 children hiding/Walter Zerla), (boy hiding/Image
Source), (boys hiding/JGI/Jamie Gril), (girl hiding/Hadi Nurseha/EyeEm),
8 (chef/Andresr), (zookeeper/Serxgio Pitamitz/robertharding), 9 (kids
with toy train/Jupiterimages), 10 (baking/Eric Audras), (skipping/swyz),
53 (market/Marc Romanelli/Stone), 78 (crowd/Ian Hitchcock), 79 (crowd/Ian
Hitchcock), 91 (cress/Dave King); **Oxford University Press** pp.13 (scouts
outside tent/David Jordan), 15 (scouts with guitar/David Jordan), 16 (boy in
green, school lunch, birthday, two girls, doctor, team coach), 19 (rabbit,
boy), 23 (aquariumMike Stone), 26(both/Mike Stone), 39 (woman, elephant,
boy), 47 (boy), 48 (koala), 48 (girl), 49 (badges, shells), 50 (teddies), 52 (teddies,
badges), 57 (boy), 67 (castle, cave house), 69 (May), 70 (castle, cave house),
75 (Zane), 76 (both), 81, 89 (both), 92 (girl watering, boys planting tree, boy
with pot), 93 (robot); **Shutterstock** pp.9 (cyclist/phBodrova), (violinist/
SpeedKingz), 10 (cycling/wavebreakmedia), (roller skating/James.Pintar),
12 (Jake/Stuart Monk), (Maria/Samuel Borges Photography), 19 (parrots/JMiks,
lizards/Pavelk), 38 (elephant/Stacy Funderburke), 39 (ducks/James Chen,
girls/Monkey Business Images), 40 (bear/Critterbiz), 44 (farmer/Goodluz, girl/
Shestakoff), 53 (soup/Nata-Lia), 69 (Jack/Valua Vitaly, Connor/Goodluz, garden/
Serg Zastavkin, door/rayisa, cat/Mi.Ti., window/Radovan, clown/Alersandr
Hunta, elephant/Naypong), 72 (garden/E. Petersen), 75 (blue house/jkirsh,
apartment block/Mika Heittola, red house/Mikael Damkier), 78 (dancer/elina),
79 (dancer/elina, elephant/Naypong), 82 (dancing/Michael C. Gray, singing/
irencik, bored), 83 (baking/Innershadows Photography, football/Wallenrock,
beach/Carlos Horta), 84 Molly/Max Topchii), 85 (Asimo/catwalker), 86 (robot/
Stokkete), 88 (girl/Pavel L), 92 (planting seedling/Jenn Huls), 93 (girl with
tomatoes/Sergiy Bykhunenko).

Commissioned photography: pp: 34, 43, 70, 77 (headshots)/Graham Alder/MM
Studios.

Contents

Billy **Gus** **Layla**  **Dot**

What Do You Know?

Verb *To be*

A Read and complete with the words in the box.

| is | are | ~~am~~ | is |

1 I ___am___ seven years old.

2 My name _____ May.

3 They _____ six years old.

4 He _____ two years old.

B Write the words in the correct order to make questions.

1 years / they / ? / Are / seven / old   Are they seven years old?

2 she / ten / old / ? / Is / years   _____

3 you / ? / old / years / three / Are   _____

4 eight / Is / old / ? / years / he   _____

C Complete the answers to the questions in **B**.

1 No, _____ aren't.

2 Yes, she _____.

3 _____, I'm _____.

4 Yes, _____ is.

D Draw a picture of you. Answer the questions.

1 What is your name?

_____

2 How old are you?

_____

Demonstratives

A Read, look, and match.

1 This is a kitten. •

2 Those are kites. •

3 That's a butterfly. •

4 These are fish. •

B Circle the correct words.

1 This (is) / **are** a boat.

2 **These** / **This** are frogs.

3 Those **is** / **are** bicycles.

4 **This** / **Those** is a train.

C Complete the sentences with the words in the box.

| Those | zebra | are | This | is | That's |

1 _____ a lion.

2 _____ is a tiger.

3 These _____ deer.

4 _____ are spiders.

5 That's a _____.

6 This _____ a peach.

There is ... / There are ...

A Complete the sentences with *There's* or *There are*.

1 _____ two kittens.

2 _____ a parrot.

3 _____ a clock.

4 _____ three crocodiles.

B Look, read, and write *yes* or *no*.

1 There's a train. _____   **3** There's a bicycle. _____

2 There are two trucks. _____   **4** There are four cars. _____

C Write the words in the correct order to make sentences.

1 erasers / five / There / are _____.

2 a / There's / giraffe _____.

3 are / pencils / There / four _____.

4 scooter / a / There's _____.

Where is ... / Where are ...

A Complete with *Where's* and *Where are*. Then match.

1 _____Where's_____ Tom?

2 _____ Mason and Lucy?

3 _____ Eva?

4 _____ Lucas, Daisy, and Tyler?

B Circle the correct words. Then match.

1 Where's / (Where) are the erasers?

2 Where's / Where are the car?

3 Where's / Where are the pencils?

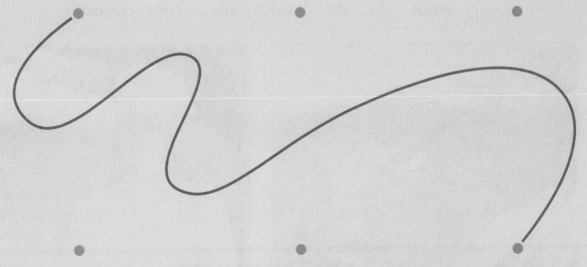

Simple Present

A **Read and check (✓) the correct picture.**

1 She works in a hospital.

2 He works in a kitchen.

3 He works in a fire station.

4 She works in a police station.

B **Complete the questions and answers with the words in the box.**

work No He works she Does doesn't

1 _____ he _____ in
a hospital?
No, he _____ .
_____ works in a zoo.

2 Does _____ work
in a fire station?
_____ , she doesn't.
She _____ in a kitchen.

Simple Present with *Have*

A Circle the correct words. Complete the sentences with the words in the box.

truck   scooter   kittens   kites

1 I have / We have _____ .

2 I have / We have a _____ .

3 I have / We have a _____ .

4 I have / We have two _____ .

B Follow and complete the sentences with *I have* or *We have*.

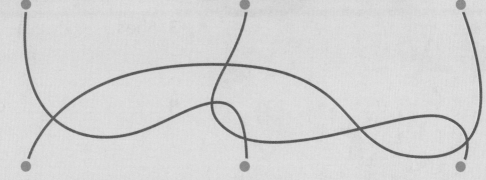

1 _____   2 _____   3 _____
a bike.   a violin.   a train.

Present Continuous

A Read and write *yes* or *no*.

1 She is roller skating. _____

2 He is reading. _____

3 He is playing soccer. _____

4 I am jumping rope. _____

B Look and complete the sentences with the words in the box.

> riding   She's   flying   He's

1 _____ playing soccer.

2 He's _____ a scooter.

3 She's _____ a kite.

4 _____ dancing.

Present Continuous Questions

A Read and circle the correct words.

1 **Are** / **Is** you running?
2 Is **you** / **Dad** reading?
3 **Are** / **Is** Mom dancing?

4 **Is** / **Are** we jumping rope?
5 **Are** / **Is** they riding bikes?
6 Is **she** / **you** buying a dress?

B Complete the questions with *Is* or *Are*. Write the answers with the words in the box.

> No, they aren't.   Yes, we are.   No, she isn't.   ~~Yes, he is.~~

1 ___Is___ he reading?

Yes, he is.

2 _____ they dancing?

_____

3 _____ you roller skating?

_____

4 _____ she playing the violin?

_____

Possessive 's

A Follow and complete with *Maria's* or *Jake's*.

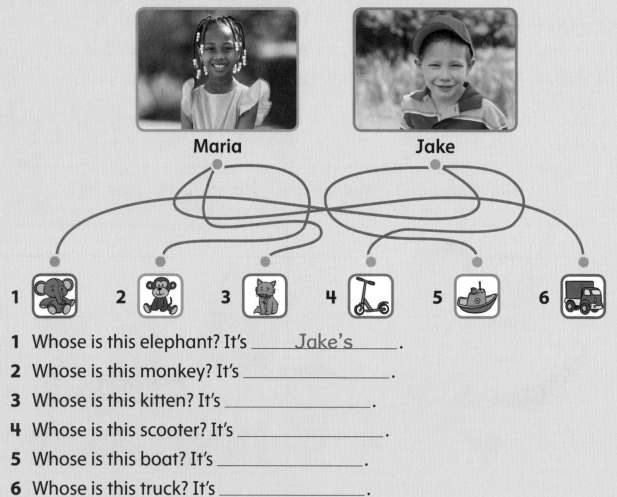

1 Whose is this elephant? It's _____ Jake's _____.

2 Whose is this monkey? It's _____.

3 Whose is this kitten? It's _____.

4 Whose is this scooter? It's _____.

5 Whose is this boat? It's _____.

6 Whose is this truck? It's _____.

B Look and complete.

1 This is Hugo's
kite.

2 _____
pens.

3 _____
bike.

4 _____
balloons.

5 _____
pencils.

6 _____
scooter.

1 A Group I Belong To

Discover Grammar

A Listen and read. 🔊 02

Hi! (I'm) Nico and I'm eight years old. I'm a boy scout! My sisters are scouts, too. They aren't boy scouts – they're girl scouts! We do different things, but we have lots of fun.

This isn't our yard. This is Mr. Howe's yard. He's old. We're young. We help him.

This is our camp. We are happy! I'm not tired! Let's play a game. Are you a scout? You can join us. You are always welcome in the scouts!

B Read the text again. Find and circle six different forms of *be*.

C Complete the text about Nico.

is	is	is not	is not	is	is

Nico ¹_____ a scout. He ²_____ a girl scout. He ³_____ a boy scout. He ⁴_____ old – he ⁵_____ young. He ⁶_____ happy!

Learn Grammar

A Read and learn.

🔍 Learn Grammar Simple Present of *To be*

Affirmative and Negative Statements

Use the verb *to be* to talk about facts.

Facts can be affirmative:

I am **a scout.**   **You** are **seven years old.**   **He** is **a teacher.**   **We** are **hungry.**

Facts can be negative:

I am not **a scout.**   **You** are not **seven years old.**   **He** is not **a teacher.**
We are not **hungry.**

Affirmative			
Full Form		**Short Form**	
I	am	I	'm
He She It	is	He She It	's
You We They	are	You We They	're

Negative			
Full Form		**Short Form**	
I	am not	I	'm not
He She It	is not	He She It	isn't
You We They	are not	You We They	aren't

B Complete the sentences.

Ella   Hi, I ¹ _____ Ella.

Sofia   Hello, I ² _____ Sofia.

Ella   Sofia ³ _____ my friend.

Sofia   We ⁴ _____ girl scouts.

C Listen and check. 🔊 03

D Act it out!

(Simple Present of *To be*: Affirmative and Negative Statements)

E **Look, read, and write *yes* or *no*.**

1 They are scouts.   yes
2 They are girl scouts.   _____
3 They are happy.   _____
4 They are friends.   _____
5 They are young.   _____

F **Read and circle the correct words.**

1 Hello. I **am** / **are** Ella.
2 This is Nico. He **'re** / **'s** my cousin.
3 We **am** / **are** scouts.

4 They **is not** / **are not** my sisters.
5 My uncle **is** / **am** a scout leader.
6 He **aren't** / **isn't** old.

G **Look and write short forms.**

1 ✗ They ___aren't___ boy scouts.
  ✓ They _'re_____ girl scouts!

2 ✗ We _____ thirsty.
  ✓ We _____ hungry!

3 ✗ She _____ my sister.
  ✓ She _____ my friend!

4 ✓ I _____ eight years old.
  ✗ I _____ fourteen years old!

H Look and complete the sentences. Use short forms.

1 He _isn't_ old.   **2** We _____ hungry.   **3** I _____ eight years old.

4 They _____ sisters.   **5** She _____ a teacher.   **6** You _____ a team.

Let's Talk!

I Look and make sentences about Ella and Nico.

		age	scout	boy scout	girl scout
Ella		9	✓	✗	✓
Nico		8	✓	✓	✗

J Tell your friend.

> Nico is eight.

> Ella isn't eight, she's nine.

K Make true sentences for you. Tell your friend.

> I / nine years old   You / my cousin
>
> She / my friend   We / boys   They / girls

> I'm not nine years old. I'm seven years old.

Simple Present of *To be*: Affirmative and Negative Statements

2 Family and Friends

Discover Grammar

A Listen and read. 04

This is Otto. Otto is lonely.
Otto sees a bird. "Hello," says Otto. "Are you my family?"

"No, I'm not. You're a parrot. Look! Those are parrots."
Otto flies to the parrots. "Hmm. These are parrots."

"Hello," says Otto. "I'm a parrot. Are you parrots?"
"Yes, we are. But we're gray parrots. We aren't your family."
"Look! That's a green parrot."

Otto flies to the green parrots.
He's happy now!

B Read the text again. Find and circle these words.

this	that	these	those

C Complete the sentences from the story.

1 This_____ is Otto.

2 Are _____ my family?

3 Look! _____ are parrots.

4 _____'s a green parrot.

5 Hmm. _____ are parrots.

Learn Grammar

A Read and learn.

Learn Grammar | Simple Present of *To be*: Yes / No Questions

You can ask questions with *be*:

Is Otto lonely?   **Are** you a parrot?   **Are** they birds?

Yes / No Questions	Short Answers	
Am I … ?	Yes, I am.	No, I'm not.
Are you / we / they … ?	Yes, you / we / they are.	No, you / we / they aren't.
Is he / she / it … ?	Yes, he / she / it is.	No, he / she / it isn't.

Demonstratives: *This, That, These, Those*

Use *this, that, these,* and *those* to show which things we are talking about.

Use *this* and *these* for things that are close.

Use *that* and *those* for things that are far away.

This is my cat.   **These are my cats.**   **That is my cat.**   **Those are my cats.**

You can use *this, that, these, those* to ask questions with *be*:

Is that your cat?   **Are these** your friends?   **Remember!** *That's = That is*

B Complete the sentences with the words in the box.

am   Are   is   That's   that

Boy   ¹ _____ you sad?

Girl   Yes, I ² _____ . I can't find my kitten.

Boy   Is ³ _____ your kitten?

Girl   Yes, it ⁴ _____ ! Thank you! ⁵ _____ Mitsy!

C Listen and check. 05   **D** Act it out!

Simple Present of *To be*: Yes / No Questions
Demonstratives: *This, That, These, Those*

E Remember the story. Match the questions and answers.

1 Is Otto lonely?   **a** No, they aren't.
2 Is Otto a dog?   **b** Yes, they are.
3 Are the gray birds Otto's family?   **c** No, he isn't.
4 Are the green parrots Otto's family?   **d** Yes, he is.

F Complete the questions with *Is* or *Are*. Then check (✓) the correct answer.

1 _____ it a cat?   ☐ Yes, it is.   ☐ No, it isn't.

2 _____ they parrots?   ☐ Yes, they are.   ☐ No, they aren't.

3 _____ he a boy?   ☐ Yes, he is.   ☐ No, he isn't.

4 _____ they birds?   ☐ Yes, they are.   ☐ No, they aren't.

G Circle the correct words.

1 **Is** / **Are** this your rabbit?   Yes, **it is** / **they are.**
2 **Are** / **Is** these your birds?   No, **it isn't** / **they aren't.**
3 **Am** / **Is** that your horse?   No, **it isn't** / **they aren't.**
4 **Are** / **Is** those your lizards?   Yes, **it is** / **they are.**

H Complete the sentences with the words in the box.

| This That These Those |

1 _____ is my horse.

2 _____ are my lizards.

3 _____ are my birds.

4 _____ is my rabbit.

Let's Write!

I Choose and draw. Write sentences with _This_, _That_, _These_, or _Those_.

| horse / horses   cat / cats   rabbit / rabbits   lizard / lizards   bird / birds |

1 _____ my _____ .

2 _____ my _____ .

3 _____ my _____ .

4 _____ my _____ .

Simple Present of _To be: Yes / No Questions_
Demonstratives: _This, That, These, Those_

Module 1 Review

A **Rewrite the sentences with short forms.**

1 She is seven years old.   <u>She's seven years old.</u>

2 I am Anna's cousin.   _____

3 He is not a boy scout.   _____

4 We are friends.   _____

5 They are not brothers.   _____

B **Look and write.**

1  (my horse / ✗)

<u>That isn't</u>
<u>my horse.</u>

2  (my lizards / ✓)

_____

_____

3  (my birds / ✗)

_____

_____

4  (my rabbit / ✓)

_____

_____

C **Read B again and answer.**

1  Is it her rabbit?

<u>Yes, it is.</u>

2 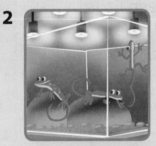 Are they her lizards?

_____

3  Is it his horse?

_____

4  Are they his birds?

_____

Discover Grammar

A Listen and read. 06

Are there animals in these photos? Yes, there are! Can you see them? Animals use color to hide.

There are two bears. They're polar bears. Polar bears live in cold places. There aren't green plants and trees. The snow is white. The bears are white.

There is a green lizard on the tree. There are green leaves. The green lizard is safe in the green leaves.

Look at the pink flowers. Is there an animal? Yes, there is! There isn't a lizard. There is a bird! The bird is yellow and pink.

B Read the text again. Underline the sentences and questions with *there is* and *there are*.

C Complete the sentences.

1 There _____ green leaves. There _____ a green lizard.

2 There _____ pink flowers. There _____ a pink and yellow bird.

3 There _____ green plants and trees. There _____ two white polar bears.

There is … / There are …

Learn Grammar

A Read and learn.

Learn Grammar — *There is … / There are …*

Use *there is* and *there are* to talk about the people and things around us.

There is **a bird in the garden.**	There are **seven frogs in the garden.**
There isn't **a bird in the garden.**	There aren't **seven frogs in the garden.**

You can ask questions with *Is there … ?* and *Are there … ?*

Is there **a bird in the garden?**	Are there **seven frogs in the garden?**

	Singular	Plural
Affirmative sentences	There is …	There are …
Negative sentences	There isn't …	There aren't …
Questions	Is there … ?	Are there … ?

Remember! *There's = There is*

B Read and circle the correct words.

Boy What's in here? ¹ **Is / Are** there an animal?

Girl Yes, ² **there is / there isn't**. ³ **There is / There are** a brown and white fish. Look!

Boy Cool! ⁴ **Is / Are** there lots of orange plants?

Girl No, ⁵ **there are / there aren't**. ⁶ **There is / There are** brown and white rocks.

C Listen and check. 🔊 07

D Act it out!

There is … / There are …

E Count and write.

Welcome to the Animal Park

1 There _is_ _one_ elephant.
2 There _are_ _____ zebras.
3 There ____ _____ lion.

4 There ____ _____ birds.
5 There ____ _____ bears.
6 There ____ _____ tortoise.

F Read, look, and match.

1 Are there seven zebras? •
2 Is there one lizard? •
3 Is there one elephant? •
4 Are there nine birds? •

• **a** No, there isn't.
• **b** Yes, there is.
• **c** Yes, there are.
• **d** No, there aren't.

G Read and circle the correct words.

1 **Is there / Are there** one tortoise?
2 **Is there / Are there** eleven lizards?
3 **Is there / Are there** three lions?
4 **Is there / Are there** one polar bear?

There is … / There are …

H Look and write short answers for **G**.

1 _____   3 _____

2 _____   4 _____

I Write true sentences about the picture.

1 seven lizards   <u>There are seven lizards.</u>

2 four polar bears   _____

3 two tortoises   _____

4 one bird   _____

Let's Talk!

J Choose and draw.

> bird / birds   elephant / elephants   tortoise / tortoises
> lizard / lizards   bear / bears   lion / lions

Animal Park

K Ask and answer with a friend.

Are there six birds?

Is there one lizard?

No, there aren't.
There are three pink birds.

Yes, there is.

Under the Ocean

Discover Grammar

A Listen and read. 🔊 08

My Favorite Place by Karima

This is the aquarium. There are lots of sea animals and fish. You can see them in the water. There's a starfish in this pool. It's on a rock. I'm next to the starfish.

The aquarium is very big and there's a tunnel! You aren't in the water – but you are under the ocean! You can see the fish through the glass. You can walk under them. Look at the beautiful turtle!

There are different areas with different fish and animals. I like the Arctic Zone, because there are polar bears.

B Read the text again. Find and circle the words in the box.

in   on   under   next to

C Look, read, and match.

1 in   3 under

2 on   4 next to

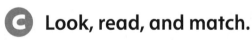
_____   _____   ___1___   _____

D Look and complete the sentences with the words in the box.

in   on   under   next to

1 I'm _____ the starfish.

2 Look! We're _____ the turtle.

3 There's a starfish _____ the rock.

4 There's an animal _____ this pool.

26 **Unit 4** Under the Ocean

Prepositions of Place: *In, On, Under, Next to*

Learn Grammar

A Read and learn.

Learn Grammar | Prepositions of Place: *In, On, Under, Next To*

Use the words *in*, *on*, *under*, and *next to* to say where people or things are.

You can use *in*, *on*, *under*, and *next to* with *be* statements and questions.

Is there a starfish **in** this pool? Yes, there is.

There's a starfish **on** a rock.

Is Karima **under** the turtle? Yes, she is.

Karima is **in** the tunnel at the aquarium.

There's a polar bear **next to** Sam.

Karima and Sam are **under** the water.

There are three turtles **on** a rock.

Are Sam and Karima **in** the water?

Are there two polar bears **next to** the tunnel?

B Complete the sentences. Circle the correct words.

Boy   Look! I can see penguins!

Girl   Are they ¹ **in** / **on** the water?

Boy   No, they ² **isn't** / **aren't**.

Girl   Oh! I can see them. They're ³ **next to** / **under** the pool.

C Listen and check. 🔊 09

D Act it out!

E Look and read. Write *yes* or *no*.

1 There are two girls on the beach. _____

2 The boy is in the water. _____

3 There is a big fish under the boat. _____

4 There's a starfish next to the sandcastle. _____

5 There is an octopus on the beach. _____

6 There are two birds on the boat. _____

F Read and check (✓) the correct box.

1 Are the girls in the boat? ◯ Yes, they are. ◯ No, they aren't.

2 Is the sandcastle under the umbrella? ◯ Yes, it is. ◯ No, it isn't.

3 Are there shells on the sandcastle? ◯ Yes, there are. ◯ No, there aren't.

4 Are there three trees on the beach? ◯ Yes, there are. ◯ No, there aren't.

5 Is there a crab next to the octopus? ◯ Yes, there is. ◯ No, there isn't.

Prepositions of Place: *In, On, Under, Next to*

G Look and complete the sentences with the words in the box.

| next to   in   on   under |

1 A boy is _____ the boat.
2 The octopus is _____ the crab.

3 The girls are _____ the umbrella.
4 There are shells _____ the sandcastle.

H Write the words in the correct order to make sentences.

1 there's / a crab / the seaweed / under _____

2 a man / the boat / in / there's _____

3 a shell / there's / the ocean / next to _____

4 on / a sandcastle / the beach / there's _____

✎ Let's Write!

I Draw and label with the words in the box.

| crab   starfish   turtle   fish |

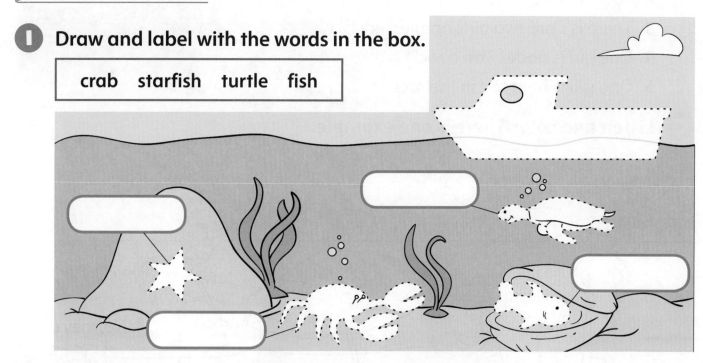

J Write sentences about **I** using the words given.

(starfish / rock)   There's a starfish on a rock _____.

(turtle / boat)   There's _____.

(crab / rock)   There's _____.

(fish / shell)   There's _____.

Module 2 Review

A Write the words in the correct order to make questions.
Complete the answers.

1 there / ? / Are / lizards / three _____

   Yes, _____

2 turtle / ? / a / there / Is _____

   No, _____

3 elephants / two / Are / ? / there _____

   No, _____

B Look and circle the correct words.

1 There **are / is** three children on the beach.

2 There is a boy **under / on** a boat.

3 There **is / are** two girls on the beach.

4 One girl is **under / on** a rock.

5 One girl is **next to / in** the rock.

C Listen and color. There is one example. 🔊 10

In the Country

Discover Grammar

A Listen and read. 11

It's fall. Hana and Grandpa walk to the pond. They watch birds and frogs. Animals drink from the pond.

Winter is snowy and cold. Hana and Grandpa take a walk. But there isn't a pond!

"Grandpa! Where's the pond?"

"It's under the snow, Hana. The winter is very cold. The water is ice."

"But … Where are the animals? Are they thirsty?"

Grandpa smiles. "The animals are in their homes. Look – there's a squirrel's nest."

"But Grandpa! Where are the frogs? They live in the water!"

"The frogs are in the pond. They're under the ice. Frogs sleep in winter."

B Read and circle the regular plurals.

> pond   frogs   squirrel   birds   animals   nest   homes

C Read the text again. Underline questions with *Where is . . . ?* and *Where are . . . ?*

D Match the questions and answers.

1 Where is the pond?   •   •   **a** They are in their homes.

2 Where are the animals?   •   •   **b** They are under the ice.

3 Where are the frogs?   •   •   **c** It's under the snow.

Where is … ? / Where are … ?

Learn Grammar

A Read and learn.

Learn Grammar — *Where is … ? / Where are … ?*

You can ask questions with *Where is … ?* and *Where are … ?* to find out the location of a person or thing.

Where is	the pond? Grandma? my cookie?		Where are	the frogs? my shoes? your books?

Remember! *Where's = Where is*

Answer *Where is / Where are* questions with *be* statements and prepositions of place.

She's in the garden.   **It's on the table.**   **They're under the ice.**
They're next to your bag.

Remember! You can ask *yes / no* questions about where things are.

Is	the pond Hana	under the snow? next to the pond?	Yes, it is. Yes, she is.	No, it isn't. No, she isn't.
Are	the animals the frogs	in their homes? under the ice?	Yes, they are. Yes, they are.	No, they aren't. No, they aren't.

B Complete the sentences. Circle the correct words.

Boy   Hi Grandpa. Where [1] **'s / are** Grandma?

Grandpa   She's [2] **in / under** the field with the goats.

Boy   Where [3] **is / are** the goats? They aren't [4] **on / in** the field!

Grandpa   Oh no! Look! They're [5] **next to / under** the road.

Boy   Oh! I need to help Grandma!

C Listen and check. 🔊 12

D Act it out!

E Look at picture 1. Match the questions and answers.

1 Where are the frogs?	●	●	**a** It's next to the pond.
2 Where is the rabbit?	●	●	**b** They're on the tree.
3 Where is the fox?	●	●	**c** They're in the water.
4 Where are the squirrels?	●	●	**d** They're on the flowers.
5 Where are the bees?	●	●	**e** It's on the grass.

F Look at picture 1. Answer the questions.

1 Are the bees in the hive?   <u>No, they aren't.</u>

2 Is the rabbit on the grass?   _____

3 Are the frogs in the water?   _____

4 Is the fox in the tree?   _____

5 Are the ducks under the water?   _____

G Look at picture 2 in **E**. Read the answers and write the questions.

| bees | frogs | rabbit | ducks | fox |

1 Where <u>are the squirrels?</u>   They're in the tree.

2 Where _____   They're under the ice.

3 Where _____   It's in the nest.

4 Where _____   They're in the hive.

5 Where _____   It's in the snow.

6 Where _____   They aren't here!

H Write the words in the correct order to make questions.

1 are / the / where / ? / bees   _____

2 rabbit / is / where / the / ?   _____

3 are / ? / where / squirrels / the   _____

4 the / where / fox / ? / is   _____

5 ? / are / frogs / the / where   _____

6 are / ? / ducks / where / the   _____

💬 Let's Talk!

I Play a game! Use the pictures on page 33.

Where are the bees?

Picture 1! Where is the … ?

They're on the flowers.

Where is … ? / Where are … ?

Who's This?

Discover Grammar

A Listen and read. 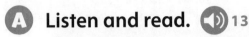 🔊 13

This is a picture of Mika and Nuraj. Mika is an elephant. Mika is very important for Nuraj's family.

Nuraj takes care of Mika. Nuraj washes Mika in the river. They play. Then it's time to work. When Nuraj eats lunch, he gives Mika food. Mika likes fruit and nuts. He loves cookies! Nuraj brings cookies for Mika.

Then, one day, Nuraj goes away. He goes to school. Mika works hard. There are no cookies. Mika is lonely.

One day after work, Mika sees something. What's this? It's a nut. Wait. What's this? It's an orange. What's this? It's a cookie. Yummy! And what's this? It's a foot. A foot? Who's this? It's Nuraj! He's home! It's the holidays!

B Look and find the words in the box in the text. Circle the words that begin with vowels.

elephant   cookie   orange   nut

C Read the last paragraph and find two different question words.

_____'s this?   _____'s this?

D Read the text again and find the answers.

What's this?   Who's this?

1 <u>It's a</u> _____ nut.   **3** _____ Nuraj!

2 _____ orange.

Learn Grammar

A Read and learn.

Learn Grammar | *What's this? / Who's this?*

You can use *Wh-* question words to ask open questions.
What … ? A question about a thing.
Who … ? A question about a person.

	Question	Answer	
Singular	What's this / that?	It's	an orange. a cookie.
	Who's this / that?		Nuraj. my cousin Leila.
Plural	What are these / those?	They're	oranges. cookies.
	Who are these / those?		my friends. my cousins.

Watch out! *Who's this? It's Nuraj.* NOT ~~*He's Nuraj*~~.

Remember! People's names have a capital letter!

Indefinite Articles: *A / An*

Use *a* and *an* with singular nouns.   **It's a cookie.**   **It's an orange.**
Use *an* before words that start with vowels.
Vowels are the letters *a, e, i, o* and *u*.   **an elephant**   **an orange**

B Suri and Nuraj are looking at a photograph. Complete the sentences.

Suri   Hi Nuraj. ¹ _____ are these children?

Nuraj   They're my cousins. They're at the zoo!

Suri   ² _____ this?

Nuraj   It's a giraffe!

C Listen and check. 14   **D** Act it out!

E Look and complete the sentences with the words in the box.

| an What's a a Who's Who's a What's |

¹_____ this?   ³_____ this?   ⁵_____ this?   ⁷_____ this?

It's Asim.
He's ²_____ boy.

It's Bina.
She's ⁴_____ girl.

It's ⁶_____ elephant.

It's ⁸_____ giraffe!

F Circle the vowels.

A B C D E F G H I J K L M N O P Q R S T U V W X Y Z

G Read and write *a* or *an*.

1 _____ ear   3 _____ eye   5 _____ arm
2 _____ foot   4 _____ hand   6 _____ nose

H Read and match.

1  •   • **a** Who's this? It's Bina.

2  •   • **b** What's this? It's a hand.

3  •   • **c** What are these? They're eyes.

4  •   • **d** What's this? It's an elephant.

5  •   • **e** Who's this? It's Asim.

6  •   • **f** What's this? It's a foot.

I Look and complete the sentences.

1 _____'s this?
It's _____ ear.
_____'s this?
It's an elephant!

2 _____'s this?
It's _____ arm. _____'s this? It's Bina!

3 _____?
It's _____ foot.
_____?
It's Asim!

4 _____?
_____ eye.
_____?
It's a giraffe!

5 _____?
_____ hands.
_____?
_____!

6 _____?
_____ nose.
_____?
_____!

✎ Let's Write!

J Number the sentences in the correct order.

☐ They're ears!

1 What's this?

☐ What are these?

☐ It's my favorite animal. It's an elephant.

K Draw your favorite animal. Write a dialogue about it.

_____?
It's my favorite animal. _____
_____?
_____!

What's this? / Who's this?; Indefinite Articles: A / An

Module 3 Review

A **Read and circle the correct words.**

1 Where **is** / **are** the boys? They **is** / **are** next to the pond.
2 Where **is** / **are** the frogs? They **is** / **are** in the pond.
3 Where **is** / **are** Dad? He **is** / **are** on the path.
4 Where **is** / **are** the fox? It **is** / **are** in the forest.

B **Complete the sentences with _a_ or _an_.**

1 It's _____ orange.
2 It's _____ tree.
3 There's _____ nest.
4 That's _____ elephant.
5 It's _____ octopus.
6 There isn't _____ giraffe.

C **Look and complete the sentences with the words in the box.**

| Who are | What are | Who's | Who's | What's |

1 _____ this?
   It's Grandma!

2 _____ this?
   It's an elephant.

3 _____ this?
   It's my cousin, Malik.

4 _____ these?
   They're ducks.

5 _____ these?
   They're my friends!

7

A Year in the Wild

Discover Grammar

A Listen and read. 🔊 15

This is a black bear. It lives in the forest. In the summer, the bear climbs trees and swims. It eats plants, fruit, and fish.

In the fall, the weather gets cool. The bear doesn't collect food for the winter. It eats a lot of food. It makes a den in the forest. Then it sleeps.

The weather gets very cold in winter. It snows. But the bear is warm in its den. It doesn't eat. It doesn't drink. The black bear sleeps for five months!

In the spring, the weather gets warm again. The bear wakes up. It's hungry and thirsty. The bear goes outside. It eats new plants.

B Find these verbs in the first paragraph. What is the missing letter?

live__   eat__   climb__   swim__

C Read the second paragraph again. Find this sentence. Write the missing words.

The bear _____ _____ food for the winter.

D Complete the sentences with the words in the box.

eat   makes   sleeps   ~~climb~~   drink

In the winter, the black bear doesn't ¹ ___climb___ trees.

It doesn't ² _____ , and it doesn't ³ _____ .

It ⁴ _____ a den, and it ⁵ _____ until the spring.

(Simple Present: Affirmative and Negative Statements with *He, She and It*)

Learn Grammar

A Read and learn.

Learn Grammar Simple Present

Affirmative and Negative Statements with *He*, *She*, and *It*

Use the simple present to talk about things that are true.

The bear lives in the forest.   **My cousin works at the National Park.**

In affirmative statements with *he*, *she*, and *it*, we add an –s to the verb.

Use the simple present to talk about habits and routines.

The bear climbs trees and swims.

With *he*, *she*, and *it*, we make negative statements with *doesn't*.

It doesn't eat in winter.

Affirmative	he	eats		Negative	he	doesn't sleep
	she	swims			she	doesn't climb
	it	sleeps			it	doesn't take

Remember! *doesn't = does not*

Use the simple present with *it* to talk about weather facts and patterns.

It gets cold in the winter.   **It snows.**

B Read and write the correct form of *work*.

Girl This is my cousin. She ¹ ✓ _____
with animals.

Boy Cool! Is she a zookeeper?

Girl No. She ² ✗ _____ at the zoo.

Boy Is she a ranger?

Girl Yes. She ³ ✓ _____ at the
National Park.

C Listen and check. 🔊 16

D Act it out!

Spring

Fall

Summer

Winter

E **Match the sentence parts.**

1 It gets hot   ●   ● snows   ●   ● in the spring.

2 It gets cool   ●   ● and sunny   ●   ● in the fall.

3 It gets   ●   ● warm   ●   ● in the winter.

4 It   ●   ● and windy   ●   ● in the summer.

F **Write the sentences. Write the season.**

1 fish / eats / bear / the

_____

_____

2 doesn't / the / collect food / bear

_____

_____

3 eat / the / doesn't / and drink / bear

_____

_____

4 plants / eats / bear / new / the

_____

_____

    Simple Present: Affirmative and Negative Statements with *He, She* and *It*

G **Remember the text! Complete a summary.**

The black bear ¹ _____ (live ✓) in the forest.

In the fall, the bear ² _____ (make ✓) a den.

The bear ³ _____ (collect ✗) food for the
winter. It ⁴ _____ (eat ✓) a lot in the fall.

It ⁵ _____ (eat ✗) in the winter.

It ⁶ _____ (sleep ✓) for five months!

H **Look and complete sentences about the park ranger's job.**

Spring:	open park ✓	eat new plants ✗
Summer:	help visitors ✓	climb trees ✗

In the spring, the park ranger ✓ _____ the park.

She ✗ _____ .

In the summer, she ✓ _____ . She ✗ _____ !

🗨 Let's Talk!

I **Imagine your sister or brother helps at the park. Check (✓) two
activities and cross (✗) two others. Then tell your partner what
your sister or brother does and doesn't do at the park.**

- ☐ help animals
- ☐ climb trees
- ☐ swim
- ☐ help visitors
- ☐ eat new plants
- ☐ work hard
- ☐ collect food

My sister helps animals.

My brother doesn't climb trees!

8

A Year on the Farm

Discover Grammar

A Listen and read. 🔊 17

Are you a farmer?
Yes, I am. I live on a farm with my family.

It's spring. Are you busy?
Yes, I am. In the spring, we plant flowers and vegetables. It's warm. The animals sleep outside.

Do you work hard in the summer?
Yes, we do. We pick strawberries. We make strawberry ice cream.

Do you pick strawberries in the fall?
No, we don't. We pick apples. We make apple pie. The weather is cool.

Do the animals sleep outside in the winter?
In the winter it's cold. The animals don't sleep outside. They sleep in the warm barn. I bring food and water to the animals. My children build a snowman.

B Read the text and circle the pronouns that you find.

I   You   He   She   It   We   They

C Read the text again and complete the sentences. Circle the correct season.

1 We _____ strawberries.   **winter / summer**
2 We _____ apple pie.   **fall / spring**
3 We _____ flowers and vegetables.   **spring / summer**
4 They _____ a snowman.   **winter / spring**

Simple Present: Affirmative and Negative Statements
with *I, You, We* and *They*; *Yes / No* Questions

Learn Grammar

A Read and learn.

Learn Grammar — Simple Present

Affirmative and Negative Statements with *I, You, We,* and *They*

Use the simple present to talk about facts, habits, and routines.

I live **on a farm with my family.**   **We** pick **strawberries.**   **We** make **apple pie.**

With *I, you, we,* and *they,* we make negative statements with *don't.*

The animals don't sleep **outside in the winter.**

Affirmative		Negative	
I / You / We / They	plant pick live	I / You / We / They	don't plant don't pick don't live

Remember! *don't = do not*

Simple Present: *Yes / No* Questions

We can ask *yes / no* questions with *Do.* Use *do* and *don't* to answer.

Do you work hard in the summer?   **Yes, I do. / No, I don't.**

Do they sleep outside the in winter?   **Yes, they do. / No, they don't.**

Question		Short Answer	
Do	I / you / we / they … ?	Yes, I / you / we / they do.	No, I / you / we / they don't.

B Complete the sentences with the verbs in the box.

pick   build   live   help   make

Girl   I'm Jenny and this is Ben. We ¹ _____ on a farm.

Boy   I ² _____ my dad in the spring.

Girl   We ³ _____ strawberry ice cream in the summer.

Boy   In the fall, we ⁴ _____ apples.

Girl   In the winter, we ⁵ _____ a snowman! The farm is fun!

C Listen and check. 18   **D** Act it out!

E Read. Then look at the pictures, and write the numbers in the boxes.

Spring ☐ ☐

Fall ☐ ☐

Summer 1 ☐

Winter ☐ ☐

1 They pick strawberries.
2 I plant flowers.
3 We make apple pies.

4 I take food to the animals.
5 We build a snowman.
6 I eat ice cream.

7 You plant fruit.
8 We pick apples.

F Circle the correct answers.

1 Do you pick strawberries in the summer?   **Yes, we do. / No, we don't.**
2 Do you take food to the animals in the winter?   **Yes, we do. / No, we don't.**
3 Do you pick apples in the spring?   **Yes, we do. / No, we don't.**
4 Do you plant fruit in the summer?   **Yes, we do. / No, we don't.**
5 Do you dig the soil in the winter?   **Yes, we do. / No, we don't.**
6 Do you make apple pies in the fall?   **Yes, we do. / No, we don't.**

G Complete the sentences with the affirmative or negative forms of the verbs in the box.

| plant   build   pick   make |

1 You _____ a snowman in the summer! You _____ a snowman in the winter.
2 We _____ apples in the fall. We _____ strawberries in the fall.
3 I _____ ice cream in the summer. I _____ apple pies!
4 They _____ flowers in the fall! They _____ flowers in the spring!

Simple Present: Affirmative and Negative Statements
with *I, You, We* and *They; Yes / No* Questions

H Look and complete Jake's text.

	Spring	Summer	Fall	Winter
	plant flowers	eat ice cream	go to school	watch fireworks
Jake	✗	✓	✓	✓
Jake's cousins	✓	✓	✓	✗

Hi, I'm Jake. My cousins live on a farm.

I don't live on a farm. I live in the city.

In the spring, they plant flowers. I [1] _____.

In the summer, we [2] _____.

In the fall, we [3] _____.

In the winter, I [4] _____.

They [5] _____.

🖊 Let's Write!

I Look and check (✓) the activities you do. Write them in the chart.

☐ eat ice cream

☐ collect seashells

☐ play in the garden

☐ go to school

☐ help Mom and Dad in the garden

☐ build a snowman

☐ swim

☐ plant flowers

☐ eat birthday cake

☐ fly a kite

Spring	Summer	Fall	Winter

J Ask and answer about the seasons with a friend.

Do you jump in the leaves?

Yes, I do. I jump in the leaves in the fall.

K Write about your favorite season. Write about the things you do, and the things you don't do.

Module 4 Review

A Read and write affirmative and negative sentences about the koala.

climb trees ✓   swim ✗   eat leaves ✓   sleep at night ✗

This is a koala.

1 <u>It climbs trees</u>_____.

2 It _____.

3 _____.

4 _____.

B Read and complete.

Spring	Summer	Fall	Winter
plant vegetables ✓	grow peas and carrots ✓ bring them to the market ✓	pick apples ✗ pick oranges ✓	work hard ✗ rest ✓

Hi! I'm Luisa. I live on a farm with my family! I like the farm.
In the spring, we [1] _____ vegetables. In the summer,
we [2] _____ peas and carrots and we [3] _____ them
to the market. In the fall, we [4] _____ apples.
We [5] _____ oranges. The orange trees are beautiful.
In the winter, we [6] _____ hard. We [7] _____!

C Match the questions and answers.

1 Do you like the farm? •   • **a** No, we don't. We plant vegetables.

2 Do you plant flowers •   • **b** No, we don't. We pick oranges!
  in the spring?

3 Do you pick apples •   • **c** No, we don't. In the winter, we rest!
  in the fall?

4 Do you work hard •   • **d** Yes, I do. I like it a lot.
  in the winter?

My Collection

Discover Grammar

A Listen and read. 🔊 19

Welcome to Collector's Corner!

Hi! I'm Lily. My sister and I collect pins. Look at our collection. I have 17 pins. My sister has 19. Together, we have 36 pins. I love pins!

Hello. I'm Diego. I collect stones and shells. I find beautiful stones and shells on the beach. My dog, Wally, comes with me. Wally doesn't have a collection, but he likes to dig!

Hello, Collector's Corner! I'm Omar and I have over 27 cars! I don't have real cars. I have toy cars. I collect all kinds of toy cars. My dad likes cars, too. He doesn't have a toy. Dad has a real car!

B Read the text in **A** again. Find and circle four forms of the verb *have*.

C Read the text in **A** again. Complete the sentences.

1 I _____ seventeen pins.

2 I _____ real cars. I _____ toy cars!

3 Dad _____ a real car!

4 Wally _____ a collection.

5 Together, we _____ 36 pins.

D Read the sentences in **C**. Check (✓) the affirmative sentences.

Learn Grammar

A Read and learn.

Learn Grammar Simple Present of *To have*

Affirmative and Negative Statements

We use the verb *to have* to talk about possessions – things that we own.
To have is an irregular verb.

We have 36 pins.   **He has a car.**

We make negative statements with *don't* and *doesn't*.

I don't have real cars.   **He doesn't have a collection.**

Affirmative	
I / You / We / They	have
He / She / It	has

Negative	
I / You / We / They	don't have (do not have)
He / She / It	doesn't have (does not have)

B Number the sentences in the correct order.

1	**Boy**	What are these?
☐	**Girl**	I have 17 teddy bears.
☐	**Boy**	How many teddy bears do you have?
☐	**Girl**	My brother has robots, too!
☐	**Boy**	I don't have teddy bears. I have robots.
☐	**Girl**	They're teddy bears. This is my collection.

C Listen and check. 🔊 20

D Act it out!

Simple Present of *To have*: Affirmative and Negative Statements

E Match the words and pictures.

1 I have a robot!

3 He has teddy bears.

5 You have seashells!

2 They have cars.

4 We have pins.

6 She has a doll.

F Read and circle the correct words.

1 We **have** / **has** lots of cars.

4 You **have** / **has** lots of teddy bears.

2 I **have** / **has** a doll.

5 They **have** / **has** pins.

3 He **have** / **has** a robot.

6 She **have** / **has** lots of seashells.

G Look, read, and check (✓) the correct box.

1 He doesn't have a teddy bear.

2 He has a car.

3 They have dolls.

4 I don't have lots of shells.

H **Read and complete with the words in the box.**

doesn't have   has   don't have   ~~have~~   have

1 You and your cousins (✓) _____have_____ lots of toys.

2 My brother and his friends (✗) _____ cars.

3 My cousin Tony (✓) _____ a big house.

4 My sister Lucy (✗) _____ lots of friends.

5 My brother and I (✓) _____ robots.

I **Read and write** *have, don't have, has,* **or** *doesn't have.*

1 ✓ Jin _____ seventeen teddy bears.

2 ✗ Her brother _____ teddy bears.

3 ✓ He _____ robots.

4 ✗ Lily and Jin _____ 36 pins.

5 ✗ Lily _____ 20 pins.

6 ✓ Lily's friends _____ pins, too.

🖊 **Let's Write!**

J **What do you have? What does your friend have? Draw and write.**

I _____ .

My friend _____ .

10 At the Market

Discover Grammar

A Listen and read. 21

Chicken soup
1 chicken
3 onions
4 carrots
2 potatoes

[At the market]

Boy	What's for lunch, Grandpa?
Grandpa	Chicken soup. What do we have at home?
Boy	Er ... We have carrots.
Grandpa	Do we have onions?
Boy	No, we don't.
Grandpa	Does that man have onions?
Boy	Yes, he does.
Grandpa	Hello. Three onions, please. And I need two potatoes. Do you have potatoes?
Man	Yes, I do. Here you go.
Grandpa	Potatoes, onions, carrots ... Chicken! Do you have a chicken?
Man	No, I don't.
Grandpa	Oh. I need a chicken for chicken soup. What do you have?
Man	I don't have meat. I have vegetables.
Boy	Does he have all the ingredients?
Grandpa	No, he doesn't ... Come on! Let's go home.

[At home. Grandpa is in the kitchen.]

Boy	It smells good! What's for lunch, Grandpa?
Grandpa	Vegetable soup!

B Read the text again. Underline questions with *have*.

C Look at the two types of questions. Match them to the answers.

1 What do we have at home? •   • **a** No, we don't.

2 Do we have onions? •   • **b** We have carrots.

Learn Grammar

A Read and learn.

Learn Grammar | Simple Present of *To have*: *Yes / No* Questions

You can ask *yes / no* questions with the verb *to have*. In the simple present, use *do* and *does* to make the questions and to answer them.

Do we have carrots?   ✓ **Yes, we do.**   ✗ **No, we don't.**

Does he have onions?   ✓ **Yes, he does.**   ✗ **No, he doesn't.**

Questions			Short Answers
Do	I / you / we / they	have … ?	Yes, I / you / we / they do.
			No, I / you / we / they don't.
Does	he / she / it		Yes, he / she / it does.
			No, he / she / it doesn't.

Remember!   *don't = do not*   *doesn't = does not*

Remember!   You can use *what* with *have* to ask open questions. *What* questions are about things.

What do we have at home?   **We have four carrots.**

What does he have for dinner?   **He has sausages.**

Remember!   *What do you have … ? → I have … / We have …*

Watch out!   *What does he have … ? → He has …*

B Read and complete the dialogue with the words in the box.

do   Do   What   have

Grandma   It's time for lunch. ¹ _____ do we have?

Boy   We ² _____ chicken.

Grandma   ³ _____ we have onions?

Boy   Yes, we ⁴ _____ . We have four onions. Let's make soup!

C Listen and check. 22   ## D Act it out!

E **Look, read, and match.**

1 What does he have for lunch? ●   ● **a** I have a sandwich and cookies.

2 What do they have for lunch? ●   ● **b** She has chicken and rice.

3 What do you have for lunch? ●   ● **c** He has soup and a banana.

4 What does she have for lunch? ●   ● **d** They have sausages
and carrots.

F **Look again at the picture above. Read and circle the correct answers.**

1 Do you have soup?   **Yes, I do. / No, I don't.**

2 Do you have potatoes?   **Yes, we do. / No, we don't.**

3 Does he have cookies?   **Yes, he does. / No, he doesn't.**

4 Does she have rice?   **Yes, she does. / No, she doesn't.**

G **Complete the answers.**

1 Does she have a sandwich?   No, _____ .

2 What does he have?   _____ a sandwich and cookies.

3 Do you have a banana?   Yes, _____ .

4 What do they have?   _____ sausages and carrots.

H **Read the answers and complete the questions.**

1 _____ for lunch?   No, I don't. I don't like soup.

2 _____ for lunch?   I have a sandwich.

3 _____ for lunch?   Yes, I do. I like chicken.

4 _____ for lunch?   He has sausages.

I **Answer the questions for you.**

1 Do you have a cookie for lunch?   _____

2 Do you have chicken for lunch?   _____

3 Do you have soup for lunch?   _____

4 Do you have a sandwich for lunch?   _____

5 Do you have a sausage for lunch?   _____

6 What do you have for lunch?   _____

Let's Talk!

J **Draw your lunch.**

K **Ask and answer with a friend.**

What do you have for lunch?   I have a sandwich.

Do you have a banana?   Yes, I do.

Simple Present of *To have: Yes / No* Questions; *What* Questions

Module 5 Review

A **Read and circle the correct answers.**

This is my friend Tom. Tom and I collect stamps.
Tom ¹ **has / have** stamps from 20 countries.
I ² **has / have** stamps from many countries, too.
We ³ **doesn't have / don't have** old stamps,
we ⁴ **has / have** new stamps. Tom ⁵ **has / have**
a friend in Egypt. He ⁶ **has / have** many Egyptian
stamps. My books ⁷ **doesn't have / don't have** Egyptian
stamps, but there are stamps from Mexico and from
China. Do you ⁸ **have / has** a stamp collection?

B **Look and complete the questions. Write answers.**

1 Do they __have__ lots of fruit?   No, they don't.

2 _____ he have carrots?   _____

3 _____ they have a chicken?   _____

4 Does she _____ two carrots?   _____

5 _____ he have two onions?   _____

6 _____ they have sausages?   _____

Discover Grammar

A Listen and read. 🔊 23

Marlon reads every day. He wants to be a teacher. But he needs new books for school.

Marlon's mom and dad work hard. They don't have money for new books. The family needs food and Marlon's brothers need school clothes. Marlon doesn't want his mom to be sad. He doesn't talk about schoolbooks at home. But he has an idea.

In the garden, there's a lemon tree. There are lots of lemons. Marlon has a little money. He buys sugar. Marlon makes lemonade. On Saturday, he makes a sign: Lemonade 50 cents.

It's hot! People are thirsty. They like Marlon's lemonade. Now Marlon has money to buy schoolbooks. He gives the rest of the money to his mom.

B Read the text again. Find and circle the verbs *have, want, need,* and *like.*

C Find these sentences. Write the missing words.

1 They _____ have money for new books.

2 Marlon _____ want his mom to be sad.

D Match the sentence parts.

1 They ●	● has ●	● school clothes.
2 He ●	● need ●	● an idea.
3 They ●	● wants ●	● Marlon's lemonade.
4 He ●	● like ●	● new schoolbooks.

Simple Present: All Forms

Learn Grammar

 A Read and learn.

Learn Grammar Simple Present: All Forms

Use the simple present to talk about facts, habits, and routines.

Marlon reads every day.   **He wants to be a teacher.**
Mom and Dad work hard.

You make negative statements with *don't* and *doesn't*:

They don't have money for new books.   **He doesn't talk about schoolbooks.**

Affirmative		Negative	
I / You / We / They	want need like	I / You / We / They	don't want don't need don't like
He / She / It	wants needs likes	He / She / It	doesn't want doesn't need doesn't like

Watch out! *To have* is an irregular verb.

I / You / We / They have	I / You / We / They don't have
He / She / It has	He / She / It doesn't have

B Read and circle the correct words.

Girl	I ¹ **need** / **needs** a new pen for school.
Boy	This store ² **have** / **has** lots of pens.
Girl	Look! I ³ **like** / **likes** that blue pen.
Boy	It's $25! You ⁴ **don't have** / **doesn't have** $25!
Girl	No. It's expensive. I ⁵ **don't need** / **doesn't need** a fancy pen.

C Listen and check. 🔊 24

D Act it out!

E **Read and match.**

1 I need an eraser. ⬭

2 I need a bag. ⬭

3 We need a book. ⬭

4 I need a pencil. ⬭

5 We need chairs. ⬭

F **Look and circle the correct words.**

1 He **need** / **needs** an eraser.

2 She **doesn't need** / **don't need** books.

3 They **need** / **needs** chairs.

4 They **don't need** / **doesn't need** pencils.

5 He **needs** / **need** a pencil.

G **Look and complete the sentences with the words in the box.**

| has   have   doesn't have   don't have |

1 He ___has___ a pencil. He ___doesn't have___ an eraser.

2 She _____ lots of books. She _____ a bag.

3 They _____ a desk. They _____ chairs.

4 They _____ pencils. They _____ a book.

5 He _____ a ruler. He _____ a pencil.

Simple Present: All Forms

H Look and complete the sentences with *have a*, *has a*, *want a*, or *wants a*, and the words in the box.

ruler   pen   chair   notebook   book   desk   bag   pencil

1 He has a _____ .

He wants a _____ .

2 She has a _____ .

She _____ .

3 They _____ .

They _____ .

4 He _____ .

He _____ .

✏ Let's Write!

I Look and check (✓) the things you have in your schoolbag. Tell a friend.

☐ ruler   ☐ eraser   ☐ book   ☐ pen

☐ pencil   ☐ computer   ☐ notebook

J Listen to your friend. Write the things your friend has.

K Write about the things you and your friend have.

In my schoolbag, I have a

_____

_____ .

My friend _____

_____ .

We need these things for school.

Discover Grammar

A **Listen and read.** 🔊 25

I'm a scientist. I study weather and animals. I live and work on this ship.

What do you have on the ship?
I have a desk and a bed. The ship has a kitchen and a bathroom. And we have games and books!

Do you need games and books?
No, we don't. But we like them! We play games in the evenings.

Does the ship have everything you want?
No, it doesn't. But it has everything we need.

What do you need?
We need food, warm clothes, and blankets. We need computers.

What do you want?
I want a hot bath. And I want to see my family!

Do you like your job?
Yes, I do. It's interesting, and it's important. We need information about our environment.

B **Read the text again. Underline the questions. Write the first words.**

1 _____   2 _____   3 _____

C **Read the answers and complete the questions.**

1 _____ you like your job?   Yes, I do.

2 _____ do you need for work?   We need computers.

3 _____ the ship have a bath?   No, it doesn't.

Simple Present: *Yes / No* Questions; *What* Questions

Learn Grammar

A Read and learn.

Learn Grammar | Simple Present: *Yes / No* Questions

You can ask *yes / no* questions with *Do* and *Does*. We use *don't / doesn't* to answer.

Do you need games and books?   ✓ **Yes, we do.**   ✗ **No, we don't.**

Does the ship have everything you want?   ✓ **Yes, it does.**   ✗ **No, it doesn't.**

We can use *do* and *does* with different verbs.

Do you want / need / like games and books?

Does she want / need / like games and books?

In short answers, we always use *do / don't* or *does / doesn't*.

Do you need a book?   **Yes, I do.**   NOT ~~Yes, I need~~.

Questions			Short Answers
Do	I / you / we / they	want … ? need … ?	Yes, I / you / we / they do. No, I / you / we / they don't.
Does	he / she / it	like … ? have … ?	Yes, he / she / it does. No, he / she / it doesn't.

Remember!   *don't = do not*   *doesn't = does not*

What Questions

You can use *what* to ask open questions. *What* questions are about things.

What do you need?   **We need food.**

What do you have?   **I have a desk.**

What does she want?   **She wants a bath.**

Watch out!   *What does he have … ?* → *He has …*

B Complete the sentences with the words in the box.

have   need   What   Do

Girl   ¹ _____ do you need for your new room?

Boy   I ² _____ a bed and a desk.

Girl   ³ _____ you have fun things?

Boy   Yes, I do. I ⁴ _____ books and games.

C Listen and check. 🔊 26

D Act it out!

E Read, look, and circle the correct words.

1 **Do / Does** he have a desk?   No, he **don't / doesn't**.

2 **Do / Does** they have computers?   Yes, they **do / does**.

3 **Do / Does** she have warm clothes?   Yes, she **do / does**.

4 **Do / Does** they have a TV?   No, they **don't / doesn't**.

5 **Do / Does** she have books?   Yes, she **do / does**.

6 **Do / Does** they have a cat?   Yes, they **do / does**.

Simple Present: *Yes / No* Questions; *What* Questions

F Match the questions and answers.

1 Hi Dad! Are you in the Arctic?
2 Do you like the ship?
3 Do you have a TV?
4 What do you have for fun?
5 What do you have for work?
6 Do you need a desk?

a No, we don't. We don't need a TV.
b Yes, I am. I'm on the ship!
c I have a computer, paper, and books.
d Yes, I do! I need a desk!
e We have games and books.
f Yes, I do. The ship is great.

G Complete the answers.

1 Does he like the ship?
  ✓ Yes, he does_____.
2 Do they need a TV?
  ✗ No, _____.
3 Do they have games?
  ✓ Yes, _____.

4 Does he need a desk?
  ✓ _____.
5 Do they like games?
  ✓ _____.
6 Does he want a pen?
  ✓ _____.

H Complete the questions with the words in the box.

| What do   Do   Does   What does |

1 _____ they have for fun?   They have books and games.
2 _____ he need for work?   He needs a computer.
3 _____ you have lots of food? Yes, we do.
4 _____ she want a TV?   No, she doesn't.

💬 Let's Talk!

I Talk about your bedroom. Ask and answer about what you have, need, and want.

Do you have a TV?   No, I don't.   Do you want a TV?   Yes, I do!

Simple Present: *Yes / No Questions; What Questions*

Module 6 Review

A Complete the sentences. Use the verbs in blue.

1 want   I ____want____ a chocolate ice cream.

My sister ____wants____ strawberry ice cream.

2 need   I _____ a red pencil.

Tariq _____ glue.

3 like   We _____ books.

They _____ TV.

4 have   I _____ red shoes.

Leila _____ blue shoes.

B Read and circle the correct words.

1 An octopus **don't / doesn't** have ten legs.

2 I **don't / doesn't** like carrots.

3 We **doesn't / don't** want chicken.

4 She **doesn't / don't** need a new computer.

5 They **don't / doesn't** have lots of games.

6 He **don't / doesn't** need an expensive pen.

C Complete the questions and answers.

1  _____ Mia want a doll?
No, she _____.
She _____ a teddy.

2  _____ Dad have blue sneakers?
No, he _____.
He _____ red sneakers.

3  _____ they need pencils?
No, they _____.
They _____ pens.

4  _____ Ali like the blue bike?
No, he _____.
He _____ the green bike.

Discover Grammar

A Listen and read. 27

Let's find out about some special homes!

This is Jack's home. He lives with his parents and his grandparents in a very big home. Jack's home is a castle! Is Jack's home old? Yes, it is.

This is May's home. May's home is a cave! May's neighbors live in caves, too. All the houses are under the ground. Is May's home special? Yes, it is.

This is Connor's home. Connor's home is a circus! He lives with his family in a caravan. Connor's aunts and uncles and cousins are in the circus, too. It's a family circus. Is Connor's home fun? Yes, it is!

B Read the text again. Find and circle the names.

C Write the possessive. Read and match.

1 Connor 's •   • a home is a castle.

2 May __ •   • b home is a circus.

3 Jack __ •   • c home is a cave.

D Read and circle the correct answer.

1 Is Connor's home fun?   **Yes, it is. / No, it isn't.**

2 Is Connor's home old?   **Yes, it is. / No, it isn't.**

3 Is Jack's home old?   **Yes, it is. / No, it isn't.**

Learn Grammar

A Read and learn.

> ### Learn Grammar — Possessive 's
>
> Add 's to the end of a name to show that something belongs to someone.
>
> **May's** home   **Connor's** aunts and uncles   **Jack's** castle
>
> We can ask *yes / no* questions about belongings with 's and the verb *to be*.
>
> Is Connor's home in a circus?   Yes, it is.
>
> Is Jack's home in a cave?   No, it isn't.
>
> Are the children's homes special?   Yes, they are.

B Complete the conversation with the answers in the box.

Yes, it is. It's fun.   No, it isn't. Jack's home is a castle.

Luca I like Jack's home.

Sam Is Jack's home a cave?

Luca ¹ _____

Sam Oh. I like the circus. Is that Connor's home?

Luca ² _____

C Listen and check. 🔊 28

D Act it out!

Possessive 's: Statements; *Yes / No Questions*

E Follow and write *May's*, *Jack's*, or *Connor's*.

1 This is _____ garden.

May

2 This is _____ cat.

3 This is _____ window.

Connor

4 This is _____ door.

5 This is _____ cousin.

Jack

6 This is _____ elephant!

F Look, read, and circle the correct words.

1 This is
May / May's.

3 This is
Connor / Connor's.

2 This is
Connor / Connor's
cousin.

4 This is
May / May's cat.

G Read the text about Jack. Write *Jack* or *Jack's*.

¹ _____ lives in a very special home. ² _____ home is a castle. ³ _____
likes the castle. It's old. ⁴ _____ grandparents live in the castle, too.
⁵ _____ loves his grandparents.

H **Read and circle the correct answers.**

1 Is this May's home?

Yes, it is. / **No, it isn't.**

2 Is this Jack's home?

Yes, it is. / No, it isn't.

3 Is this May's home?

Yes, it is. / No, it isn't.

💬 Let's Talk!

I **Complete the sentences.**

1 _____ May's home a castle?

2 _____ Connor's cousins in the circus?

3 _____ Jack's home a circus?

4 _____ the homes in May's street in caves?

5 _____ Jack's home very old?

J **Remember the text. Ask and answer with a friend.**

Is May's home a castle?

No, it isn't. May's home is a cave.

Possessive 's: Statements; *Yes / No Questions*

Home Sweet Home

Discover Grammar

A Listen and read. 29

Ned is a donkey. He lives in a field. Next to his field, there are two donkeys.

"Their field is fun," thinks Ned, "My field is boring."

He jumps over the fence. The donkeys are fun, but they're noisy! Ned sees another field.

He jumps over. The field is quiet, but it's small. Ned is hungry. Ned sees a bird in the next field.

"Its field is big," thinks Ned. He jumps over. The bird flies away. Ned is lonely.

Ned jumps into the road. The road is busy. He sees a nice, quiet field.

"That field is quiet," thinks Ned. He jumps into the field.

"Wait! This is my field! My field is nice!"

Now Ned is happy in his field!

B Read the text again. Circle these possessive adjectives.

| my | his | its | their |

C Read and match.

1 Ned's field   • their field

2 the field with two donkeys •   • its field

3 the bird's field   • my field

Possessive Adjectives: *My, Your, His, Her, Its, Our, Their*

Learn Grammar

A Read and learn.

Learn Grammar | Possessive Adjectives

| my | your | his | her | its | our | their |

These are possessive adjectives. They tell us who owns something.

This is a field. It's my field. It isn't your field. It's our field!

We also use possessive adjectives to talk about friends and family.

My sister is ten.   **This is my friend Jake.**   **His dad is a farmer.**

And when we talk about parts of our bodies.

I wash my hands.   **Did you hurt your finger?**

Possessive adjectives change. They match the owner, not the thing.

Jack's **book**	his **book**
Lucy's **dolls**	her **dolls**
Jack and Lucy's **house**	their **house**
the dog's **ball**	its **ball**

I	you	he	she	it	we	you	they
my	your	his	her	its	our	your	their

We can ask *yes* / *no* questions with possessive adjectives.

Is her field noisy?   **Yes, it is. / No, it isn't.**

Is your house big?   **Yes, it is. / No, it isn't.**

B Read and circle the correct words.

Girl   You have a great yard. Is that ¹ **your** / **their** swing?

Boy   No, it's my sister's swing. It's ² **his** / **her** favorite toy!

Girl   I don't have a yard. ³ **My** / **Its** home is an apartment.

Boy   Well, we can share – this can be ⁴ **our** / **their** yard!

C Listen and check. 🔊 30

D Act it out!

    (Possessive Adjectives: *My, Your, His, Her, Its, Our, Their*)

E Look and write the letters. Then read and circle the correct words.

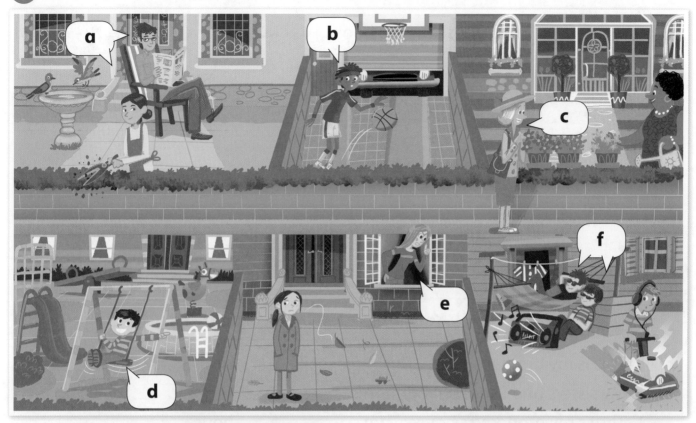

1 [b] **My / Her** yard is small.

2 [ ] **Their / My** yard is noisy!

3 [ ] **Our / Its** yard is quiet.

4 [ ] **Her / My** yard is boring.

5 [ ] **His / Your** yard is beautiful.

6 [ ] **My / Our** yard is fun.

F Look and complete the sentences with the correct words.

1 Is _____ yard noisy? No, it isn't.
  a her   **b** his   **c** our

3 Is _____ yard noisy? Yes, it is.
  a my   **b** her   **c** their

2 Is _____ yard boring? No, it isn't.
  a her   **b** his   **c** our

4 Is _____ yard big? No, it isn't.
  a their   **b** her   **c** your

Possessive Adjectives: *My, Your, His, Her, Its, Our, Their*

G Read and match.

1 These are his books.

2 This is its toy.

3 This is her book.

4 These are their toys.

H Complete the sentences with the words in the box.

| my | Your | his | her | our | their | its |

1 This is my brother's swing. This is _____ swing.

2 My sisters and I share a room. This is _____ room.

3 That's my grandma's house. That's _____ house.

4 Mr. and Mrs. Lewis live next to me. They are _____ neighbors.

5 The dog has a ball. This is _____ ball.

6 You have a nice garden. _____ garden is nice.

7 Those boys like music. Listen, _____ music is loud!

✏️ Let's Write!

I Read the text and write the possessive adjectives.

My home, by Laura

I live in an apartment. ¹ __My__ building is big and white.

I live with ² _____ mom, ³ _____ dad, and ⁴ _____ sister.

I share a room with my sister. ⁵ _____ room is nice.

J Write about your home, your family, and your room.

I live in _____ . _____ home is _____ .

I live with _____ . _____ room is _____ .

Possessive Adjectives: *My, Your, His, Her, Its, Our, Their*

Module 7 Review

A Read and complete with possessive adjectives.

Hi, I'm Zane.

My grandpa's home is special. ¹_____ home is a boat!

I live in the city with my parents. ²_____ home is an apartment. It's great!

My aunt Lisa and uncle Ben's home is big. ³_____ home is pretty. It's blue.

My friend Lily's home is small. ⁴_____ house is red. I like it.

B Read and check (✓) the correct answers.

1

Is this Zane's home?

⬜ Yes, it is.   ⬜ No, it isn't.

3

Is this Zane's home?

⬜ Yes, it is.   ⬜ No, it isn't.

2

Is this Grandpa's home?

⬜ Yes, it is.   ⬜ No, it isn't.

4

Is this Lily's home?

⬜ Yes, it is.   ⬜ No, it isn't.

C Read and write *Zane's* or *Grandpa's*.

1 _____ home is in the city.

2 _____ home is in the countryside.

3 _____ home is an apartment.

4 _____ home is a boat.

Having Fun at the Parade

Discover Grammar

A Listen and read. 31

Dear Diary,

It's bed time, but I'm not sleeping. It's a holiday in my town, and I'm waiting for the big parade! I'm in our apartment. I'm sitting next to the window, and I can see the street. Lots of people are on the street. They aren't working. They are having fun.

A woman is selling pancakes and candy. They smell good! Many people are buying them.

I can hear music. A man is playing a big drum. Children are dancing and people are singing.

Now Mom is watching, too. She is smiling and singing. I'm not singing! I'm clapping. The festival is fun!

B Read the text again. Find and circle the *-ing* forms of these words.

clap sleep sit dance sing smile wait buy

C Match the beginnings and endings to make sentences.

1 Mom is …   •   • **a** sleeping.
2 A man is …   •   • **b** dancing.
3 They aren't …   •   • **c** smiling and singing.
4 Children are …   •   • **d** playing a big drum.
5 I'm not …   •   • **e** working.

Present Continuous: Affirmative and Negative Statements

Learn Grammar

A Read and learn.

Learn Grammar | Present Continuous

Affirmative and Negative Statements

Use the present continuous to talk about the things that people are doing now.

I am writing **in my diary.**   **Mom** is singing.

We can talk about what people aren't doing now, too.

I'm not sleeping.   **They** aren't working.

Form the present continuous with the verb *to be*, and the *-ing* form of the main verb:

Affirmative			Negative		
I	am / 'm	singing. sleeping. eating. buying.	I	am not / 'm not	singing. sleeping. eating. buying.
You	are / 're		You	are not / aren't	
He / She / It	is / 's		He / She / It	is not / isn't	
We / They	are / 're		We / They	are not / aren't	

Watch out! Watch out for spelling!

With most verbs we just add *-ing*:   *sing**ing**   eat**ing**   sleep**ing***

With verbs that end in a silent *e*, we drop the *e* and add *-ing*:

make → making   have → having

With verbs that end in a short vowel + a consonant, we double the last letter and add *–ing*:

sit → sitting   clap → clapping

B Complete the sentences.

Boy   Listen! The band ¹ _____ playing!

Girl   The parade ² _____ coming!

Boy   Can you see our friends?

Girl   Yes, they ³ _____ dancing.

Boy   Look at Nick. He ⁴ _____ playing the drum!

C Listen and check. 32   **D** Act it out!

E Read and complete the sentences with the words in the box.

She He I We It They

1 There's a tall man. _____ is walking.

2 We're in the band! _____ are playing music.

3 Can you see me? _____ am playing the big bass drum!

4 There are eight girls. _____ are dancing.

5 There's an elephant. _____ is eating peanuts.

6 The carnival queen is happy. _____ is smiling.

F Look, read, and match. Then write *'m*, *'s*, or *'re*.

1 You _____ eating ice cream.

2 I _____ dancing!

3 They _____ clapping.

4 He _____ playing music.

 1

G Write the words in the correct order to make sentences.

1 dancing / I'm / not _____

2 aren't / we / eating _____

3 are / watching / they _____

4 he / smiling / is _____

Present Continuous: Affirmative and Negative Statements

H **Complete the sentences with affirmative or negative continuous forms. Use the verbs in blue.**

1 sing

She isn't singing.

2 play

I _____ a big drum.

3 eat

It _____ peanuts.

4 walk

He _____.

5 dance

They _____.

6 clap

You _____.

✏ Let's Write!

I **Look at Lizzie's picture and complete her text.**

We're at the parade!

My friend _____. (✓ dance)

I _____. (✗ dance)

I _____. (✓ clap)

J **Imagine you are at the parade. Choose two verbs. Draw yourself and your friend.**

| dance   sing   watch   eat   clap   play the drum |

We're at the parade!

My friend _____.

I _____.

I _____.

16 The Homemade Orchestra

Discover Grammar

A Listen and read. 🔊 33

Narrator	Danny is in the kitchen. What a noise!	**Danny**	Are you shaking your jars?
Mom	Danny, what are you doing?	**Oscar and Fay**	Yes, we are!
Danny	I'm finding things! I need jars and paper.	**Danny**	Are you striking your drums?
Narrator	Danny's friends come to his house. What a noise!	**Kate and Evan**	Yes, we are!
Danny	Oscar, are you making a shaker?	**Danny**	Are we making music?
Oscar	Yes, I am.	**All**	Yes, we are! We're making music and we're having fun!
Danny	Kate, are you making a shaker?		
Kate	No, I'm not.		
Danny	What are you making?		
Kate	I'm making a drum!		
Narrator	Listen! Danny and his friends are practicing their instruments!		

B Read the text again. Underline questions with the present continuous.

C Remember the story. Read and match.

1 Danny, what are you doing?   ● ● **a** I'm making a drum.

2 Kate, are you making a shaker?   ● ● **b** Yes, they are!

3 What are you making?   ● ● **c** I'm finding things.

4 Are they practicing their instruments?   ● ● **d** Yes, we are!

5 Are we making music?   ● ● **e** No, I'm not.

(Present Continuous: Yes / No Questions; *What* Questions)

Learn Grammar

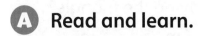

A Read and learn.

Learn Grammar | Present Continuous: *Yes / No* Questions

We can ask *yes / no* questions with the present continuous:

Is he singing?   **Are they** practicing?   **Am I** making a shaker?

We answer present continuous questions with *be*.

No, he isn't.   **Yes, they** are.   **Yes, I** am.

Questions			Short Answers		
Am	I		Yes, No,	I	am. 'm not.
Are	you		Yes, No,	you	are. aren't.
Is	he / she / it	singing?	Yes, No,	he / she / it	is. isn't.
Are	we / you / they		Yes, No,	we / you / they	are. aren't.

We can ask open questions with *what*. Answer open questions with present continuous sentences.

What are you doing?   We're playing our instruments.

What are you making?   I'm making a drum.

B Number the sentences in the correct order.

☐ **Boy** Are you using a jar?

[1] **Boy** What are you doing? Are you making a drum?

☐ **Girl** Yes, I am. Look. I'm using a jar and some beans.

☐ **Girl** No, I'm not. I'm making a shaker.

C Listen and check. 🔊 34   **D** Act it out!

E **Complete the sentences with the correct words.**

1 ____ your brother playing the drum?

   a Is   **b** Am   **c** Are

2 ____ your mom and dad listening?

   a Is   **b** Am   **c** Are

3 ____ the boys singing?

   a Is   **b** Am   **c** Are

4 ____ she playing the triangle?

   a Is   **b** Am   **c** Are

5 ____ you dancing?

   a Is   **b** Am   **c** Are

6 ____ we making music?

   a Is   **b** Am   **c** Are

F **Match the questions and answers.**

1 What are you doing?   ●   ● **a** She's making a shaker.

2 Are you having fun?   ●   ● **b** No, he isn't.

3 Is he practicing his instrument?   ●   ● **c** We're practicing for the show!

4 What is she making?   ●   ● **d** Yes, they are!

5 Are they making music?   ●   ● **e** Yes, we are!

G **Write the words in the correct order to make questions.**
Then write short answers.

1 you / are / playing / the drum?

_____

_____

3 are / singing? / they

_____

_____

2 dancing? / she / is

_____

_____

4 fun? / he / having / is

_____

_____

(Present Continuous: *Yes / No Questions; What Questions*)

H **Read the answers. Write questions. Use the verbs in blue.**

1 do   <u>What are you doing?</u>   I'm smiling and clapping.

2 make   _____   He's making a shaker.

3 sing   _____   We're singing a great song!

4 play   _____   They're playing drums.

5 watch _____   I'm watching a great show!

Let's Talk!

I **Look at the verbs in the box. Choose an action, but don't say.**

sit on the beach   play the drum   sing a song   play football
make a cake   dance   swim   eat an ice cream   climb a tree

J **Read the dialogue. Practice with a friend.**

What are you doing?   Guess!

Are you playing the drum?   No, I'm not.

Are you making a cake?   Yes, I am!

K **Choose a verb and act it out. Take turns. Ask and answer with a friend.**

What are you doing?   Guess!

Are you climbing a tree?   No, I'm not.

A Complete the text with affirmative and negative forms of the present continuous.

Dear Pedro,

Your vacation in a castle is cool! I'm happy you ¹ _____ ✓ (have) fun.

We ² _____ ✗ (stay) in a castle!

We ³ _____ ✓ (visit) my grandparents.

And I ⁴ _____ ✓ (sleep) in a tent in the yard! It's great.

My brother Danny ⁵ _____ ✗ (watch) TV.

He ⁶ _____ ✓ (play) outside.

Mom and Dad ⁷ _____ ✓ (sit) in the yard, too!

See you soon,

Alice

B Write the words in the correct order to make questions.

1 staying / Is / in a castle? / Alice _____

2 Is / sleeping / in a tent? / Alice _____

3 TV? / Danny / watching / Is _____

4 playing / Is / outside? / Danny _____

5 Are / sitting / in the yard? / they _____

C Answer the questions in **B**.

1 No, __she isn't__ .   3 No, _____ .   5 Yes, _____ .

2 Yes, _____ .   4 Yes, _____ .

Robots

Discover Grammar

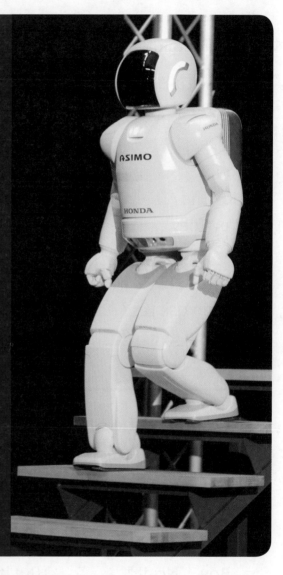

This is Asimo. Asimo is a very special robot.

Can robots walk?

Many robots can't walk. Asimo can walk and run. It can climb up stairs. Asimo can dance and kick a ball, too!

Can Asimo hear?

No, it can't. Asimo can't hear music. It can dance because it can copy people.

Can Asimo speak?

Asimo can say some words, but it can't learn like you can. You can think. Asimo can't think.

Can Asimo eat?

Asimo can't eat and it can't drink. But it can pour a drink for you! Asimo can help people. It is a robot helper for people who can't do some things.

B Read the text again and circle *can* and *can't*.

C Check (✓) or cross (✗) the things that Asimo can and can't do.

- ☐ walk
- ☐ hear
- ☐ drink
- ☐ dance
- ☐ kick a ball
- ☐ run
- ☐ say words
- ☐ think
- ☐ move
- ☐ eat

Learn Grammar

A Read and learn.

Learn Grammar *Can:* Affirmative and Negative Statements

We use *can* to talk about ability. We use *can* before a verb to talk about the things that we are able to do.

You can **think.**   **It** can **kick a ball.**

We use *can't* (*cannot*) before a verb to talk about the things we are not able to do.

Asimo can't **hear.**   **It** can't **eat and drink.**

I		move.
You	can	dance.
He / She / It	can't	sing.
We / They		run.

Look! *Can* and the main verb always stay the same.

We can ask *yes / no* questions with *can*.

Can you dance?   **Can they sing?**   **Can he move?**
Yes, I can.   **No, they can't.**   **Yes, he can.**

B Complete the sentences with *can* or *can't*.

Boy   Look! This is my robot.
Girl   Cool. ¹ _____ it move?
Boy   Yes, it ² _____ . Look. It has wheels.
Girl   Oh. ³ _____ it walk and run?
Boy   No, it ⁴ _____ . But it ⁵ _____ make music.
          Listen!

C Listen and check. ◀)) 36

D Act it out!

Can: Affirmative and Negative Statements; *Yes / No* Questions

E **Look, read, and circle the correct words.**

1 It **can** / **can't** hear the music.
2 He **can** / **can't** dance.
3 She **can** / **can't** drink.

4 The robots **can** / **can't** eat.
5 The boys **can** / **can't** smile.
6 They **can** / **can't** kick a ball.

F **Match the questions and the answers.**

1 Can Asimo walk? ●
2 Can all robots run? ●
3 Can robots eat? ●
4 Can the boy dance? ●
5 Can the boys smile? ●

● **a** Yes, he can. He can hear the music.
● **b** Yes, they can. They are having fun.
● **c** No, they can't. Asimo is special.
● **d** Yes, it can. It can walk and run.
● **e** No, they can't. Robots don't need food.

G **Look and complete the sentences.**

1 It _____ copy.

3 It _____ run.

2 It _____ eat and drink.

4 It _____ smile.

H Write the words in the correct order to make sentences.

1 move / can / the / robots   <u>The robots can move.</u>
2 the stairs / it / climb / can't   _____
3 can / it / with the ball / play   _____
4 can / smile / the / children   _____
5 can't / the / robots / dance   _____
6 children / can / the / run   _____

I Write questions about the robots. Use the verbs in blue. Then complete the answers.

1 run   <u>Can the robots run</u> ?   No, they can't.
2 move   _____ ?   Yes, they can.
3 play   _____ ?   Yes, _____.
4 smile   _____ ?   No, _____.

✏ Let's Write!

J Read and check (✓) the things that you can do.
☐ play football   ☐ swim   ☐ ride a bike   ☐ make a cake
☐ eat an ice cream   ☐ sing a song   ☐ dance   ☐ ride a bike

K Tell a friend.

Can you ride a bike?   No, I can't. But I can swim!

L Write two things that you can do, and two things that you can't do.

I can _____ .

_____

I can't _____ .

_____

But I can learn!

18 In the Garden

Discover Grammar

A Listen and read. 🔊 37

How To Grow Sunflowers

1 Buy young plants. You should choose small, green plants. You shouldn't buy plants with yellow leaves.

2 Get some pots. Remember: sunflowers grow tall! You should choose big pots. You can use old pots, but you shouldn't use dirty pots.

3 You should put some small stones in the pots. Then put the soil in the pots.

4 Make holes in the soil and put in the plants. You should give them lots of water.

5 You should choose a sunny spot for your flowers. They need to be in the sun for seven hours every day.

6 Check the soil. Is it dry? You should water the plants. Plants need water to grow.

B Read the text again. Underline advice with *should* and *shouldn't*.

C Remember the text. Circle the correct answers (*a* or *b*).

1 Should I choose plants with yellow leaves?

   a Yes, you should.   **b** No, you shouldn't.

2 Should I choose small pots?

   a Yes, you should.   **b** No, you shouldn't.

3 Should I put soil in the pots?

   a Yes, you should.   **b** No, you shouldn't.

4 Should my sunflower grow in a sunny spot?

   a Yes, it should.   **b** No, it shouldn't.

5 Should I give my plants lots of water?

   a Yes, you should.   **b** No, you shouldn't.

Learn Grammar

A Read and learn.

Learn Grammar | *Should* for Advice

We can use *should* and *shouldn't* to give people advice.

✓ You **should** buy small, green plants.

✗ You **shouldn't** buy plants with yellow leaves.

I		choose …
You	should	buy …
He / She / It	shouldn't	plant …
We / You / They		clean …

We can ask *yes* / *no* questions with *should*, to ask for advice or opinions.

Should I buy young plants?   **Yes, you should.**

Should I choose small pots?   **No, you shouldn't.**

B Match the questions and answers.

1 Should I plant some ●
  strawberries?

2 Should I plant them ●
  under this tree?

3 OK. Now, should ●
  I water them?

● **a** No, you shouldn't.
  They need the sun.

● **b** Yes, you should.
  They need water.

● **c** Yes! I like strawberries.

C Listen and check. 38   **D** Act it out!

Should for Advice: Affirmative and Negative Statements; *Yes* / *No* Questions

E Look, read, and number. Then check (✓) the correct answers.

1 Should I use a big pot?

☐ Yes, you should.   ☐ No, you shouldn't.

2 Should I choose a plant with yellow leaves?

☐ Yes, you should.   ☐ No, you shouldn't.

3 Should we give the plants water?

☐ Yes, we should.   ☐ No, we shouldn't.

4 Should I plant my sunflower here?

☐ Yes, you should.   ☐ No, you shouldn't.

5 Should I clean this old pot?

☐ Yes, you should.   ☐ No, you shouldn't.

F Complete the sentences.

How to make a cress head

1 ✓ You _____ clean a jar or plastic pot.

2 ✓ You _____ draw a face on the pot.

3 ✗ You _____ use soil. Use wet cotton balls instead.

4 ✓ You _____ put lots of seeds in.

5 ✓ You _____ find a sunny spot for your cress head.

6 ✗ You _____ let your cress head get dry.

7 ✓ You _____ take a picture and send it to your grandma!

G Write the words in the correct order to make sentences. Then match them to the pictures.

1 the tree / should / in a sunny spot. / we / plant _____

_____

2 she / water / should / the flowers. _____

3 shouldn't / put / close together. / you / the plants _____

_____

4 choose / shouldn't / he / a small pot. _____

H Read the questions. Complete the answers.

1 Should I grow lots of fruit and vegetables?   Yes, _____.

2 Should we plant tomatoes in winter?   No, _____.

3 Should they pick all the flowers?   No, _____.

4 Should she choose a small, green plant?   Yes, _____.

💬Let's Talk!

I Read and match the problems and the advice.

1 The soil is dry.   ●   ● **a** You shouldn't plant a sunflower here.

2 This is a dark corner. ●   ● **b** You should clean it.

3 This pot is dirty.   ●   ● **c** You should water your plants.

4 This pot is small.   ●   ● **d** You should choose a big pot.

J Act out the dialogues. Ask and answer with a friend.

> The soil is dry!   You should water your plants.

Should for Advice: Affirmative and Negative Statements; Yes / No Questions

Module 9 Review

A Complete the sentences with *can* or *can't*.

1 ✗ It _____ swim. 4 ✗ It _____ hear.

2 ✓ It _____ dance. 5 ✗ It _____ sing.

3 ✓ It _____ move. 6 ✓ It _____ help.

B Write the words in the correct order to make questions.

1 you / can / dance? _____

2 they / hear? / can _____

3 can / swim? / it _____

4 can / move? / they _____

5 she / sing? / can _____

6 he / a bike? / can / ride _____

C Answer the questions in **B**.

1 ✓ Yes, _____ I can _____ . 4 ✓ _____

2 ✗ No, _____ . 5 ✗ _____

3 ✗ _____ 6 ✓ _____

D Complete the sentences with *should* or *shouldn't*.

Let's grow tomatoes!

1 ✓ You _____ choose small, green plants.

2 ✓ You _____ plant them in a warm place.

3 ✓ You _____ give the plants lots of water.

4 ✗ You _____ pick the green tomatoes.

5 _____ I water the plants in the day?   No, you 6 _____ .

7 _____ I eat the tomatoes when they're red?   Yes, you 8 _____ .

Grammar Reference

Simple Present of *To be*

Use the verb *to be* to talk about facts.

Affirmative		Negative	
I	am	I	am not
He / She / It	is	He / She / It	is not
You / We / They	are	You / We / They	are not

You can ask questions with *be*.

Yes / No Questions	Short answers	
Am I … ?	Yes, I am.	No, I am not.
Are you / we / they … ?	Yes, you / we / they are.	No, you / we / they are not.
Is he / she / it … ?	Yes, he / she / it is.	No, he / she / it is not.

Simple Present: Affirmative and Negative Statements

Use the simple present to talk about facts, habits, and routines.

Affirmative		Negative	
He / She / It	eats / swims / sleeps.	He / She / It	does not eat / swim / sleep.
I / You / We / They	eat / swim / sleep.	I / You / We / They	do not eat / swim / sleep.

Simple Present: *Yes / No* Questions

We can ask *yes / no* questions with *Do* and *Does*. We use *do / does* and *do not / does not* to answer.

Yes / No Questions		Short Answers
Do I / you / we / they	want … ? need … ? like … ?	Yes, I / you / we / they do. No, I / you / we / they do not.
Does he / she / it		Yes, he / she / it does. No, he / she / it does not.

Simple Present of *To have*

Use the verb *to have* to talk about possessions – things that we own.

To have is an irregular verb.

Affirmative		Negative	
I / You / We / They	have	I / You / We / They	do not have
He / She / It	has	He / She / It	does not have

We can ask *yes / no* questions with *have*. In the simple present, we use *do* and *does* to make the questions and to answer them.

Questions	Short Answers
Do I / you / we / they / have … ?	Yes, I / you / we / they do. No, I / you / we / they do not.
Does he / she / it have … ?	Yes, he / she / it does. No, he / she / it does not.

Possessive 's

Add 's to the end of a name to show that something belongs to someone.

May's home.

Possessive Adjectives

Possessive adjectives tell us who owns something.

This is a field.   It's my field.   It isn't your field.   It's our field!

We can ask *yes / no* questions with possessive adjectives.

Is her dog noisy?   Yes, it is. / No, it isn't.

Subject Pronouns	Possessive Adjectives
I	My
You	Your
He	His
She	Her
It	Its
We	Our
You	Your
They	Their

Present Continuous

Use the present continuous to talk about the things that people are doing now.

We form the present continuous with the verb *To be*, and the *–ing* form of the main verb.

Affirmative		Negative	
I am		I am not	
You are	singing.	You are not	singing.
He / She / It is		He / She / It is not	
We / They are		We / They are not	

We can ask *yes / no* questions with the present continuous.

Questions		Short Answers	
Am I		Yes, I am.	No, I am not.
Are you		Yes, you are.	No, you are not.
Is he / she / it	singing?	Yes, he / she / it is.	No, he / she / it is not.
Are we / you / they		Yes, we / you / they are. No, we / you / they are not.	